the disappearing self

the disappearing self

poems

Mickey J. Corrigan

Cover design by Shay Culligan

Cover Photograph by Arnold Arluke, Luke Arnold Photography;
model Bunny Wilford

ISBN: 978-1-950462-63-6

Kelsay Books Inc.

kelsaybooks.com

502 S 1040 E, A119
American Fork,Utah 84003

Acknowledgments

Poems appeared in the following publications, some in slightly altered form:

Fauna Quarterly: "Opening," "Everywhere Sea and Sky," "Until Death"
Scrittura: "Like Words on a Liquor Bottle"
Alt Lit Press: "Shotgun Man"
Red Fez: "Grande," "Red Tide"
Work to Calm: "Sea Change," "Happy Lastday"
Ars Medica: "Triaging Your Life"
Transcendental Visions: "Late Stage Accounting," "Drinking School"
Ink, Sweat & Tears: "Insignificance"

Contents

"There isn't nearly enough nothing in the world anymore."
—The North Pond Hermit

"You're the last person I will love
You're the last face I will recall
And best of all, I'm not gonna miss you
Not gonna miss you"
—Glen Campbell, *I'm Not Gonna Miss You*

Late Spring Melt

In your late ambitious stage
your mileage shows
you make the best of it
raw fear hard raging
in your darkline eyes.

After sundown, cold.

You bring one back
for warmth
your place
a squat foreclosure
candlelit, scattered lamps
draped in bright scarves
shoplifted from Target.

Whatever else
things turn out to be
fine
is not one of them.

High on lusty wine
yourself
going, gone
you skate the bedroom
weave into the unfamiliar
embrace, another attempt
to fool yourself
the ice will hold.

Next day humiliation
enfolds you
like a lover's arms.
You are on thin ice
all the way to wherever
hard drinks are poured,
lost time forgotten.

Marine Life

Below the rough surface
you know who you are:
a sandbar stumble
men thrust themselves on
for survival,
pull out too early
for life to go on.

Stuck in a dirty aquarium
in overdrive mode
bluing undertow
sucks you under,
your sad bloat
tasting of atrophy.

Life as last call.

Before you disappear
again
in another amber glass
you debate self-prescription
a short reach for the box
rusty razor blades
free with every case
of hundred-proof self-loathing.

Youth: the odds were good
even if the goods were odd.

Remember the deep dives
swept along
by fervency and lust?
Now it's all the same

a natural disaster chain
tsunamis of loss.

Tide's out
wet suits cling
blackened bodies doing
the dead fish float.

Through the Shutters

Early morning light
glimmers of slivers
sharp blue slicing
naked skin.

There is consciousness,
then consciousness
of consciousness.

A broad sun scorches
leafing trees
bouncing harsh gleam.
Your sunglasses go on
'til nightfall.

Up and down the sand
in the city, on freeways
steaming, overheated
you know what you're doing
saving yourself up
for something else
waiting for it
always waiting
disappearing
that kind
of self-betrayal.

Black starless nights bring
casual sweeps of salt
breeze off the wild waves
crashing, hard landings
scrape flesh from bone
making you conscious
of desire

to escape
what you think
of yourself, all women
wait for the dark
to take them.

Opening

At the cemetery gate,
in the crowded café:
a face like a daisy in bloom.

This is a person. She is
not yet white credits,
end screen blackness.

Your catharsis bleeds through her
easy
like sunlight or sweat.

In the obligatory night scene
violence follows harsh-lit love-
making, flesh smacking flesh.

The audience waits for this.
She gives them what they want.

This is a person. She is
not who you
not who they
imagine.

This is beauty,
petals bright as summer,
weeping pollen
dusting all
bystanders, voyeurs
party to a brief moment

of blush, inevitable fade.

City Nights

Skeletal cranes shoot up
above adolescent towers
and in the train station
arched doorways
frame a fat yellow moon.

Sluts and slammers dance
the chessboard floor. Bent
crones drag suitcases
stuffed with old regrets.

A time window opens
onto your former self
there, on a battered bench
younger, red lipped and hippy
full head of dropdead hair.

Castanets and carnations
the pucker of small limes
hot sauce dripping
down the wrists of strange men.

Why didn't you grab
the fleeting moment
of your unavailability?
Stay pure, stay yourself?

Instead, you let go
gave and gave
your self,
covering vast distances
sweet ripe to old age.

And here you are now
in a dimmed moonlight
sneaking sips from a brown bag
your limbs weakened
bones ashed to dust.

Nightshades

Darkness forms a potato
mask you wear
when eyes go blind.

Asparagus stockings,
shoes that burn off
in this half world where
things only half happen,
none matter.

Enter the empty egg carton
pocket windows sealed,
foundation charred
unable to hold weight.

There's little you can buy
in this aisle or that,
nothing with prayer
to save you.

Prices are reduced
to a distant   place
you only want
to leave   you
behind.

Bury your waste
d   e   e   p
as if organic life
never happened.

Like Words on a Liquor Bottle

You tell yourself:
Drink and forget.
Don't drink and drive
him
away.

Let yourself sink now
below the waves of blankness
and return by empty boat
floating down the slope of his shoulder
to settle in the pool of his broad chest.

You are a full dose
the packaging tells all
nothing is missing
all the ingredients
on the surface
deep inside
where they've always been.

Whatever lurks
behind the printed words
outside the spattered mirror
beyond the opaque glass
the amber flow
the unspoken all
the paradox of loving
a way of life
until death do you
drink, please

don't drink

alone.

What to Do Post Sell Date

Take yourself off the shelf,
out of the realm of desire.
Strip off the plastic, the bling,
fake smile. Toss the bombs.
The revolution failed—it was
loose limbed, unfashionable
based on cheap accessories.

No more consumer chic.
Now you belong
to yourself.
You don't have to behave,
stay in compliance,
not anymore.

Slack off
the wax, the buff, the personal
this and that.
You can fit back inside
your own body,
say no
to submission
to an impossible aesthetic
that starves
hurts
lies.

Take a look at yourself
in the funhouse mirror.
Note everything
you still like
about yourself.
Keep saying no.
You won't kneel

lie
down
in the anthology of shame.

Wear purple
walk the hard streets
without heels, with confidence
nobody's looking.

You made the buy
yourself.

Everywhere Sea and Sky

Today's ocean rough-handed,
you could use a bigger boat
in such a hurl of crushing surf.
Escapee fleeing
your own disappearance
you sink fast,
a wreck.

Above you, fast clouds
sail across the tangerine moon,
roughshod
in an enormous hostile sky.

Somehow you wash up,
sand sticky on your palms.

The tiny island suits you.
Coconuts fall, break open.

Lime-hued parrots in troops,
downshift
squawking
onto seagrape branches.
The flock's overcrowded
cranky, but as one.

Later they explode
in a black thunder
of winter crows,
transformed
while you looked elsewhere.

You are immersed in harsh,
violent metaphors
for your own life.

Squeezed by circumstance,
then scattered
catapulted so casually
to a distant shore.

Rules of Distraction

The train leaves the station
a flurry of hissing grind
you glide ahead
mind at ease
not knowing
not ever knowing.

At the fork
tracks beckon
you have to choose
between loving
and being loved,
disappearing
and being alive.

In the long dark
tunnel
you must pass through
an absurd frenzy
of desire
to broadcast yourself
despite a bleak lack
of receivers.

At the next station
the crowd surges, eases back
like the swollen tide.

Over and over
the same lesson:
do something good
nobody cares;
do something bad
and get rewarded.

Off the rails
back on again.
Toss yourself over
hold yourself back.

When you stand up
finally
with your liquor bottle
your juicy flesh
your guns blazing

the gods hush

the train keeps moving.

Tindered

At the dark dawn
of your new elegance
heeled high
silked, shaved, shined
with a touch of gold

you sit straight, attentive
across starched linen
while he orders the 1962,
the 10-ounce, the stuffed...

You preen and lean in
but he doesn't see
the effort
the expense
the need
he goes on and on
you smile, listen, listen...

You are your own
deletion.

Fine wine
rich food
coffee and desert
you serve your time
he stores himself in you

you are the small white hospital
for his bloated self.

Triage or sex
ICU or I don't.
Makes no difference

to you
tonight

invisible
as always.

Willed Pursuit

He could tell
you wanted it
tossing your hair
breasts through lace
breath thick with drink.

He told his friends
you asked for it
all that plastic
blood lips and nails
the sleek glitter
on a bar stool
so late at night.

You didn't say no
cool hand on his arm
the way you smiled
when he bought a round.

He could tell
you knew
what he wanted
from you, sitting alone
a woman, alone.

They just know
you want it
even when you say
you don't.

And you?
You didn't want
him. But you did

want
something.

He gave you
something

to cry about.

Shotgun Man

living in a shotgun house.
Sawed off little plug
in a neighborhood fulla
shotguns, blast pocked
with black-smoke holes.

Toilets on the front lawn
blowaway dirt
to the chain-link fence.
Scrawny dogs
snout-prowl cocky roosters.
Mangy cats on rust-out cars.
No white buds
on the dogwoods.
Blown out lights
on the saggy porch.

In the darkness you feel
that stiff breeze
from the coldhearted world.
It's not California.
Nobody cares down here.

You're on the redneck Titanic.
Not nearly
enough lifeboats
or places to land.

But with him,
you tell yourself
you feel it
allover.
Hot sand tongue,
leather hellshirt

slop-happy lust.
Shotgun blasts
between the thighs, breasts
pert up, hard
to let that kind of thing go.

Goldman Sachs and the Nikkei,
pressed slacks and a retirement fund,
such shit don't turn you,
don't matter no more.

Not when you're loving
a shotgun man
in a shotgun house
in a shotgun world.

Grande

Big lips, big tits, big ass
and a wash of big hair
she was smiling at him
in that way and
it took
about thirty seconds
before he was
what he thought was
in love
with what he thought was
her.

He was about as
easy
to get as
a bad cup of coffee
at the diner
where she sashayed
back and forth, that kind
of tempting dish.

And the mere possibility
that she might be
swinging a hip his way
lit him up,
was all
it took
to arouse
his interest.

He smiled at her
in that way
and that's all
it took

for her
to take him home
and eat him up
and drink him dry.

Thirty years later and
she's big as their house
big mouth, big fights
and he wishes he was
hard
to get
as a smile
from the sexy barista
at Starbucks.

Ex

Armed with long arrows, a bow
you go hunting
through the woods of his mind.
You regret not shooting him
between his small black eyes.

When he takes you fishing
in a glass bottom boat
you see his shallow depths.
You regret not shoving him
watching him sink
like a ball and chain.

You go for a ride
a mule team trek
across the desert of your love
hot sand whipping
everything dry,
barren.
You regret not leaving him
without a canteen,
his goddam flask.

He's asking for it
all your friends say.
You bring him to a vegan dinner
where the other guests
hollow eyed and brittle
snap him like a carrot.

You devour him together
kiss licking
your blood swelled lips.

Sea Change

When the red moon rises
and tides rip the shoreline
pukka shells are cast
black pods and debris
swept in with African winds,
                         only then
should you go out,
walk to the bar
barefoot
long hair in your eyes
long bone in your fist
thighs rubbing like coins
wide hips that sway
like a ship on a wave

so he won't miss you
nobody will miss you

not the boys in flowered board shorts
lean frames in low doorways,
the drunks in dirty sandals
asleep on slatted benches,
brown kids shirtless, on skateboards,
school girls half naked
watching through hooded eyes.

Let them all see you
emerge from the darkness
an eclipse, a sun splash
on sidewalks still warm
from the day, their hard feet
the life that stretches out
before them to the ocean
                    because now

you are full
of outcast light
this world another dream
your lure going deeper,
your last bright buoy
silver flask at your lips.

Red Tide

Like a drowning man
in love with the wild surf
he spent time with another
sucking him
under, deeper, riptides
of push and pull lust.

You couldn't hold him
to your shifting shore.
You'd been there before.
This time he washed away.

And you? You drifted off
plugged into the primitive parts
of other nervous systems
to charge and recharge
some other self.

White squalls built
in your placid waters
and you capsized
over and over.

When you woke up
in someone else's bed
someone else's body
someone else's life
you knew:
no going back.

You kept the sheets pressed
at home
his bed warm
yourself open

for him. But you knew:
he was lost
so blissfully lost

so you poured yourself
in the blood red sea.

The Day After the Day After

Alone on the bench
hair tangled seaweed
face lobster-raw as if
a bandage just ripped off
bluing up here and there
you stare out at the ruffles
the sea stirring itself slowly
for another day of tranquility.

Passersby glance down
at the lump of a suitcase
all your worldly belongings
donated sweaters
dirty underwear
an old picture frame
wrinkled yellow photo
a dream you once had.

The skateboarders say hello
beach walkers drop folded dollars
in an upturned Panama hat.

A woman stops, tsks, says
hit him back next time.
There is no next time,
you're gone.

You watch them saunter
surf, laze, laugh
unaware of the beauty
the natural teal-blue wave
upon wave upon wave
of contentment
that is their wallowing
in the salt-licked serenity
of an ordinary day.

The Last Affair

Darkness shrouds your car
and speeds you toward your future
and there you are, locked in
the glove compartment of your mind.

Lonely women are bored women.

You speak to him softly
in the passive cellphone voice
while his big warm hands
caress his wife's lean limbs.

Bored women are impulsive women.

Scars healed white
on your wrists, thighs, throat
your fingers throb and twitch
to open them up again.

Impulsive women are trouble.

He can't see you now?
That's what he thinks.

Triaging Your Life

It is not a high wire act
not a rock concert after-party
on speed.
You are out of context and it shows
in your deep rose bloom
the sad whites of your eyes.

The labcoats rush by
Starbucks in hand,
stethoscopes flying
heels click across tile.
No time
to stop dancing, ask
how does it feel
to be you in crisis.

It is not an Oscar handed down
generation after generation.
First woman to win
the Nobel Prize for weepery.

It is not a one act play
starring Ellen Burstyn and Meryl Streep
and you
are not the spotlit crystal centerpiece.

No, this is a lying ovation
the sharp sound
of one small hand clapping,
the waiting room in stitches
you cracking them up.

You *are* the crisis.

It is the anger you carry with you
always, who you carry it for
the one inconstant.

Before the drunk, the fight
the burly cops
the broken tooth and ribs and lacerations,
before the ambulance
the butt shot, restraints
at the last decent coffee bar in the city
it was just you
and a nice hot grande
black, with sugar.

It wasn't your fault.

You are a crisis
behind any curtain.

Pick one.

Rx: You

Bones, X-rays, facts
scattered to the wind
in a rash gust of spring.

Today you flip
glossy magazine pages
showing you how to live.

Life is anti-
climactic. You throw down
and the hospital corridor
shimmers like glass.

White coats, white pills
white noise in your head.
A boredom so monumental
it humbles you.

Sip whiskey, watch TV
mimic a normal person;
adjust the dream
tone it down, please.

Ask yourself this: what is
your obligation
to the truth?

This is a medical test
you will not pass.

Late Stage Accounting

Six women
one old hotel suite
two magnums,
black bottles sparkling
in fading summer light.

Between you
three divorces
four foreclosures
five children
too much
ADD, addiction, depression,
disappearance, loss.

A leering moon
slips from the leafy hills
above a gleaming river.
Towering ash, blond birch
thick woods unchanged
since college.

Down on Main Street
dirty kids in ripped jeans
cross-legged with guitars.
The same folk ballads
anti-war
pro-love.

Six girls hiked green mountains
wearing the world like a red dress.
Six girls who wanted everything
settled for what they got.

Multiply them by half a billion.
You do the math.

Until Death

When the wound blooms
flowering into its own body
and you enter it,
enter into the hurt
no longer moving ahead
slowly
like blood drawn
through a glass tube
instead, you surge
full-on, pump yourself
around and around
feel every lost corpuscle
splat out of you
feel every blued bruise
well and pool
on your hot flesh.

This is what you mean
about pain and orgasm
you suffer together
interconnected
chain links
in the chokehold collar
holding you fast
to this raw scrape earth
you drag yourself across
until you are planted
six feet below
the rest of them,

the rest
of the walking wounded.

Insignificance

The sea that bears you
agitated today
frosted with creamy froth
whitecaps
rushing headlong
at the ragged shore.

You are one small wave
surrounded
by your own kind.

The land does not notice you
no matter what color
you may offer:
yesterday
a brilliant turquoise,
today
a crush of silvered blue.

The land has lost interest
in you
when you cough yourself up,
drag along the endless sand.

You are one small wave
in an ocean of many oceans.
This is the best
you can hope for,
the best you can do.

Happy Lastday

You make a map of your death
so you have something
to leave
your children.

You've decided to slip
into something
more comfortable.

You become the long silence,
you are the creator
of that silence.

Your arms crisscross
over your hollowed chest
like spoons on a dessert dish
after dining is done.

Your see your death
as a flat state
all plains, tall weeds
you drive through
on your way elsewhere.

You wear engraved stone
draped over bones, ash.
You make it look good.

Dead is the new sixty.
Sixty is the new black.

You may get past it
but you'll never
be the same.

Drinking School

Behind the gritty park
in the ranky tunnels
where the local bums hung out
that's where you learned
to take it
any way they'd give it to you

The booze rode shotgun
everywhere you drove
top down, strange
hands in your pants

The Irish way

In a cocktail shaker
of grace
and savagery
you survived

There are no metaphors
for it:
you survived

Men, marriages, beatings
hospitals
bars, bins, bottles stashed
where you couldn't find them

No hair of the dog
all the fur scraped
from your tongue
you tell bedtime stories
to your wide-eyed grandkids
while sipping cold tea
from a stained glass.

About the Author

Mickey J. Corrigan lives in South Florida within walking distance of too many beach bars. Her novellas and novels have been published by small presses in the US, UK, Canada, and Australia. Her poetry chapbooks include *The Art of Bars* (Finishing Line Press, 2016), *Days' End* (Main Street Rag, 2017), and *Final Arrangements* (Prolific Press, 2019).

Visit at www.mickeyjcorrigan.com.